BY PAMELA DELL

The Child's World®

Published by The Child's World®
1980 Lookout Drive • Mankato, MN 56003-1705
800-599-READ • www.childsworld.com

Acknowledgments
The Child's World®: Mary Berendes, Publishing Director
The Design Lab: Design
Jody Jensen Shaffer: Editing
Red Line Editorial: Photo Research

Photo credits
Bkephoto /iStock.com: cover, 1; Eric Isselee/Shutterstock.com: 22-23; Geri Lynn Smith/Shutterstock.com: 9; GVictoria/Shutterstock.com: 5; iStock/Thinkstock, 19; Joe Belanger/Shutterstock.com: rope; John S. Sfondilias/Shutterstock.com: 16; Kenneth William Caleno/Shutterstock.com: 6; L.E. Mormile/Shutterstock.com: 12; MBoe /Shutterstock.com: 20; Michelle Marsan/Shutterstock.com: 15/ Paul McKinnon/Shutterstock.com: 11; Vaclav Volrab/Shutterstock.com: horseshoes

ISBN 9781626870048
LCCN 2013947283

Printed in the United States of America
Mankato, MN
July, 2014
PA02237

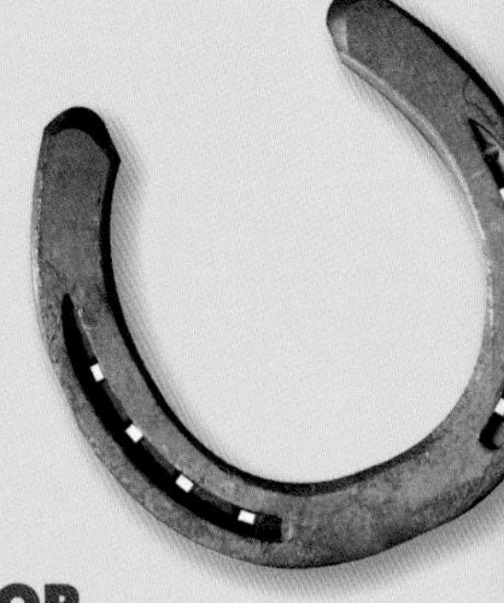

ABOUT THE AUTHOR

Pamela Dell is the author of more than fifty books for young people. She likes writing about four-legged animals as well as insects, birds, famous people, and interesting times in history. She has published both fiction and nonfiction books and has also created several interactive computer games for kids. Pamela divides her time between Los Angeles, where the weather is mostly warm and sunny all year, and Chicago, where she loves how wildly the seasons change every few months.

CONTENTS

The Powerful Clydesdale

A team of mighty horses prances down the street. These huge horses are pulling a big wagon easily. They are exciting to watch. Their manes are braided. Their short tails are neatly tied up. Their steps are high, quick, and smooth. Only one **breed** of horse looks and moves like this—the Clydesdale!

Clydesdales first came from Lanarkshire, Scotland. Lanarkshire used to be called Clydesdale. The River Clyde flows through this area.

Clydesdales had simple beginnings. They were **draft horses** used for hard work. They plowed farmers' fields. They pulled big wagons and carts.

Clydesdales have come a long way since then. They are no longer just powerful helpers. Today, people love them for many reasons.

These Clydesdales are pulling a group of people on a hayride.

What Do Clydesdales Look Like?

Clydesdales stand out in any crowd! They are big, heavy horses. In fact, they are one of the biggest draft horses. A horse's height is measured at its **withers**. Many Clydesdales measure over 6 feet (almost 2 meters) high. They weigh close to 2,000 pounds (907 kilograms).

A horse's height is measured in hands. A hand is 4 inches (10.2 centimeters). Many Clydesdales are around 18 hands high. That means they are 6 feet (almost 2 meters) tall.

These powerful horses are built for hard work. They have long, strong legs. Their hooves are huge. One hoof is about 11 inches (23 centimeters) across. That is as big as a dinner plate!

How big are Clydesdales' hooves? They are twice the size of Thoroughbred racehorses' hooves!

You can see the size of this Clydesdale's hooves.

Clydesdales are prized for their beauty, too. They are usually brown or **bay**. Sometimes they are black, gray, **chestnut**, or **roan**. Most Clydesdales have white on their faces and legs. Most of them have black manes and tails. They all have long, flowing hair on their lower legs. This long hair is called feather.

Clydesdales are known for their lively, high-stepping **gait**. As they walk, they lift their hooves high. Their long feather swings with each step. Their necks have a beautiful curve. Clydesdales have a flashy look people love!

A Clydesdale lifts its foot high with every step. From behind, you can see the whole bottom of its hoof.

This Clydesdale has been groomed for a parade.

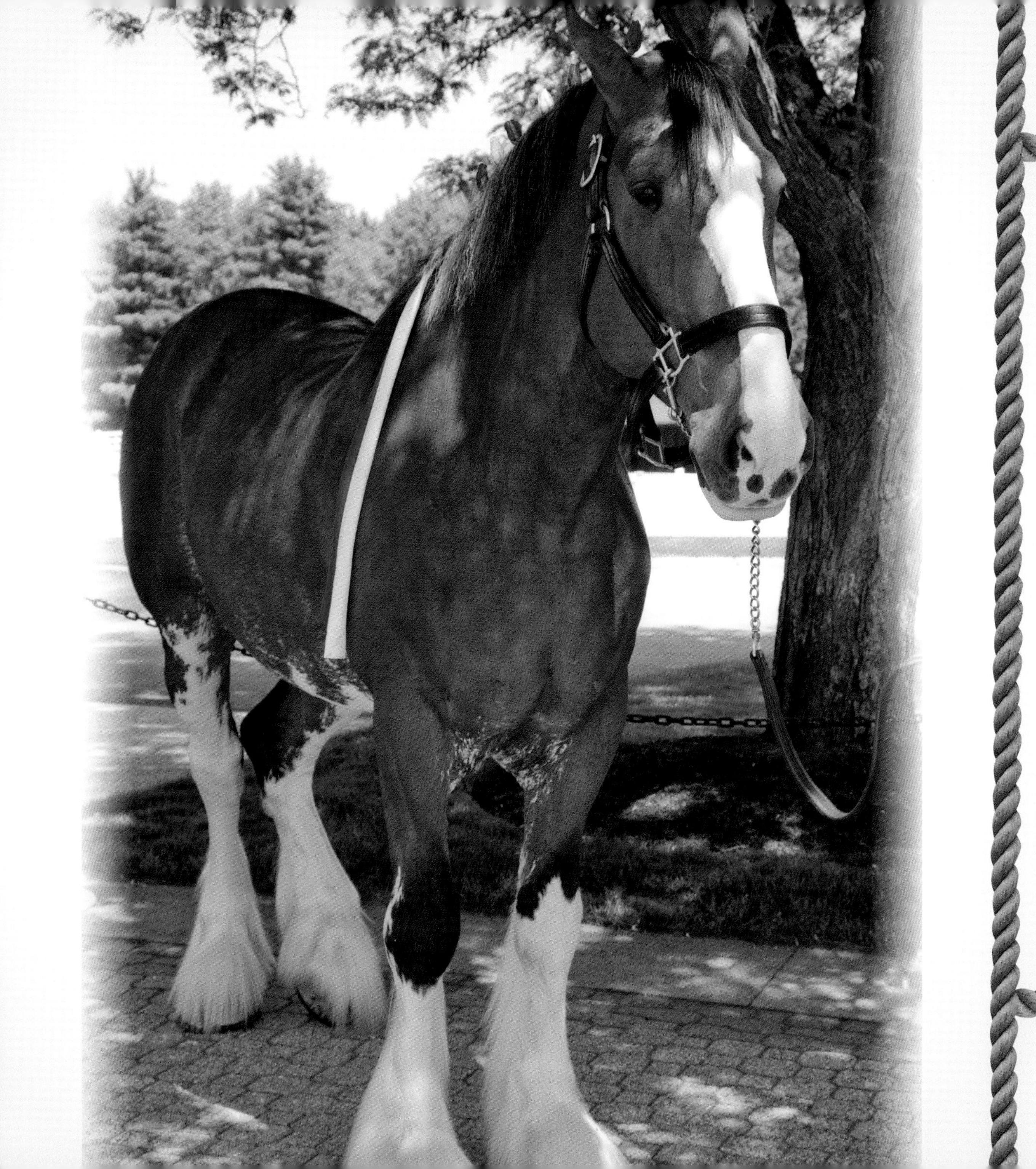

Newborn Clydesdales

A newborn Clydesdale is a leggy little horse! At birth, its legs are nearly as long as its mother's. Standing up for the first time is not easy. The **foal** struggles to its feet. It can walk when it is only a few hours old. And it wants to eat right away!

A Clydesdale mother makes lots of milk for her foal. She might make 100 pounds (45 kilograms) of milk a day!

For its first six months, the foal stays close to its mother. It drinks its mother's milk and grows quickly. At birth, it is only about 42 inches (a little over 1 meter) tall. It weighs about 125 pounds (57 kilograms).

The foal grows fast in its first few months. It might put on 4 pounds (almost 2 kilograms) a day! At four years old, the horse is fully grown. Most Clydesdale foals do not change color as they grow. But babies born with a mousy gray-brown color are different. Most newborns this color turn black later on.

This Clydesdale mare is protective of her young foal.

Clydesdales in History

The Clydesdale breed goes back some 300 years. Clydesdales are a mix of other kinds of horses. People in Clydesdale already had draft horses. Then they brought some bigger horses from Flanders. Flanders is now part of Belgium and the Netherlands. These new horses came from a breed ridden by knights. Knights wore heavy armor. They needed big, powerful horses.

The big Flemish horses and the Scottish horses had babies. These foals were spirited, strong, and beautiful. They became the first Clydesdales.

The Clydesdale breed developed over many years. These horses were good for farm work. They pulled wagons, carts, and plows. In the 1800s, they pulled heavy loads of coal. Soon they were used on city streets. People liked their fancy gait. They used them to pull **carriages**.

Clydesdales are the national horse of Scotland.

These Clydesdales are working together to plow a field.

In the late 1800s, people brought Clydesdales to North America. But American and Canadian farmers liked other horses better. The Clydesdales' feather got too dirty in the fields. Their big hooves squashed new plants. The Clydesdales became mostly city horses.

In the cities, people noticed these big horses. They noticed their quick, smooth gait. Often, teams of Clydesdales pulled big wagons. But in the early 1900s, people started using cars and trucks. The cars and trucks soon took the place of horses. Clydesdales were almost forgotten.

After cars and trucks became common, the number of Clydesdales dropped. For a while, the breed was in danger of dying out.

In the 1930s, one company brought Clydesdales back again. Clydesdales once pulled the company's wagons. Now trucks were doing that job. But the company hooked Clydesdales to shiny new wagons. They put them in their ads. People loved to see the big horses. The company is still known for its Clydesdales.

People love to see Clydesdales in parades.

What Are Clydesdales Like?

Clydesdales have a nickname—Gentle Giants. They are gentle and friendly. When they stand together, they touch and rub against each other.

These horses are always willing to work hard. They are quiet and easy to handle. Farm children can tell them what to do. Even on busy streets, Clydesdales stay calm. Horns, shouts, and other loud noises do not make them panic.

Clydesdales might be calm, but they are never boring! They are fun to watch in shows or parades. You can see their lively spirit.

Clydesdales have sensitive taste buds! They can tell the difference between salty things and sweet things.

These Clydesdales are calmly enjoying some grass in a field.

Clydesdales at Work

Trucks, tractors, and other big machines are everywhere. They have taken over the heaviest work. But in some places, draft horses are still important. Clydesdales still pull plows and wagons on some farms. They are still important for farm work in Ireland.

Many Clydesdales still work in Argentina. Up to 12 horses might pull a single wagon.

Some Clydesdales work in forests. They work where foresters cannot use tractors.

Mostly, people have Clydesdales because they enjoy them. The horses do some lighter work. In some places, they still pull carriages. In Hawai`i, they pull wedding carts carrying the bride and groom. Some Clydesdales travel to be in parades and shows. Clydesdales still draw a crowd wherever they go!

These two Clydesdales are hard at work pulling a plow.

Clydesdales Today

Once, Scotland had well over a hundred thousand Clydesdales. Today, there are only a few thousand in the world. The largest number live in North America. Others live in England, Scotland, Wales, and Ireland. Still others live in South Africa, Australia, and New Zealand.

One company, Anheuser-Busch, has the biggest herd of Clydesdales in the world—over 200 horses!

There is good news for people who love Clydesdales. More people are learning about these excellent horses. The number of Clydesdales is growing!

Today, you do not see many Clydesdales on city streets—except in parades. You might see some in farm fields or on country roads. But they are still favorites at fairs and horse shows. People love to see these big horses and watch them move. And seeing these gentle giants in person is best. They are a sight you will never forget!

Most Clydesdales live for about 18 to 23 years.

Clydesdales are calm, gentle horses.

Body Parts of a Horse

1. Ears
2. Forehead
3. Forelock
4. Eyes
5. Nostril
6. Muzzle
7. Lips
8. Chin
9. Cheek
10. Neck
11. Shoulder
12. Chest
13. Elbow
14. Forearm
15. Chestnut
16. Knee
17. Cannon
18. Pastern
19. Coronet
20. Hoof
21. Barrel
22. Fetlock
23. Hock
24. Tail
25. Gaskin
26. Stifle
27. Point of hip
28. Croup
29. Loin
30. Back
31. Withers
32. Mane
33. Poll

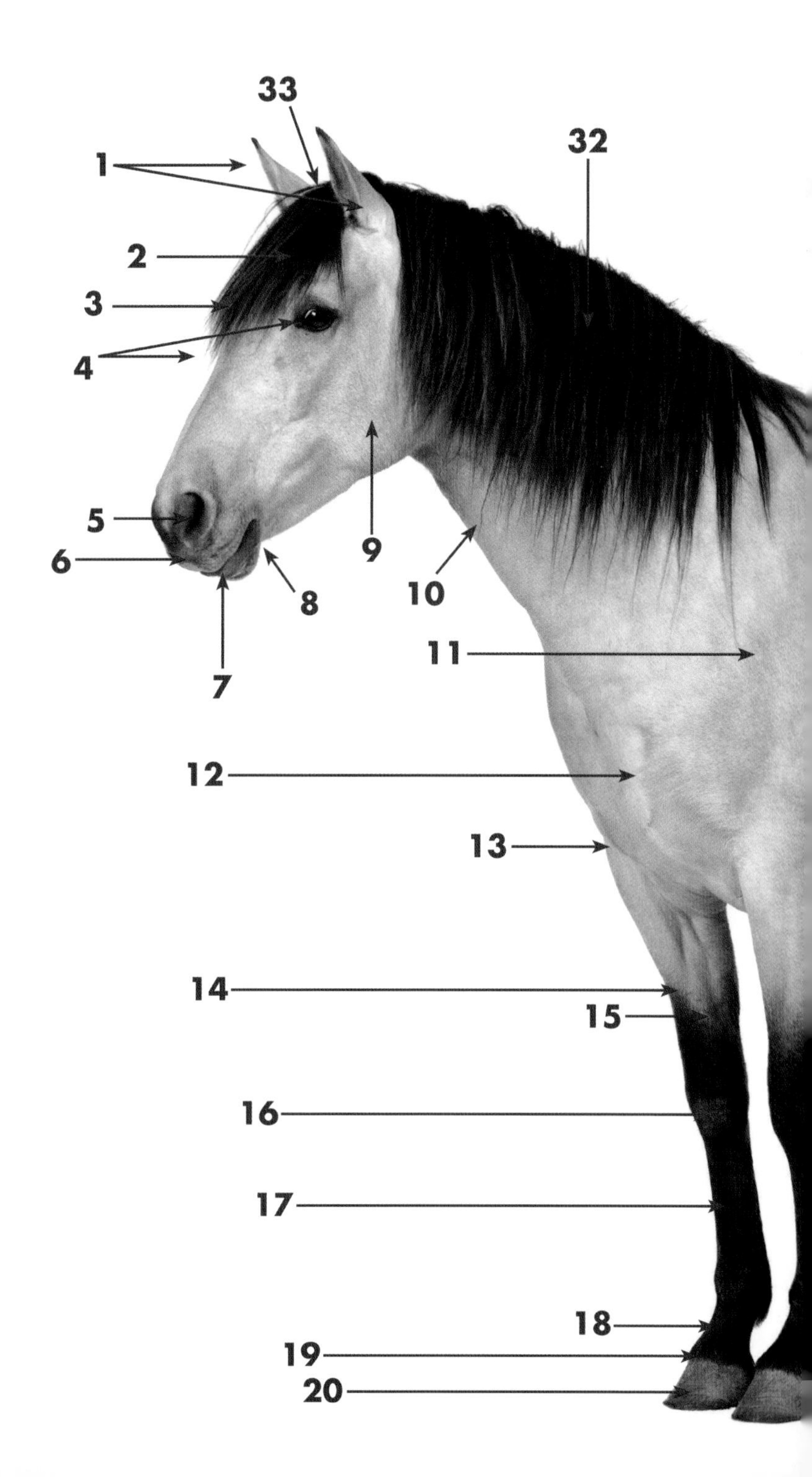

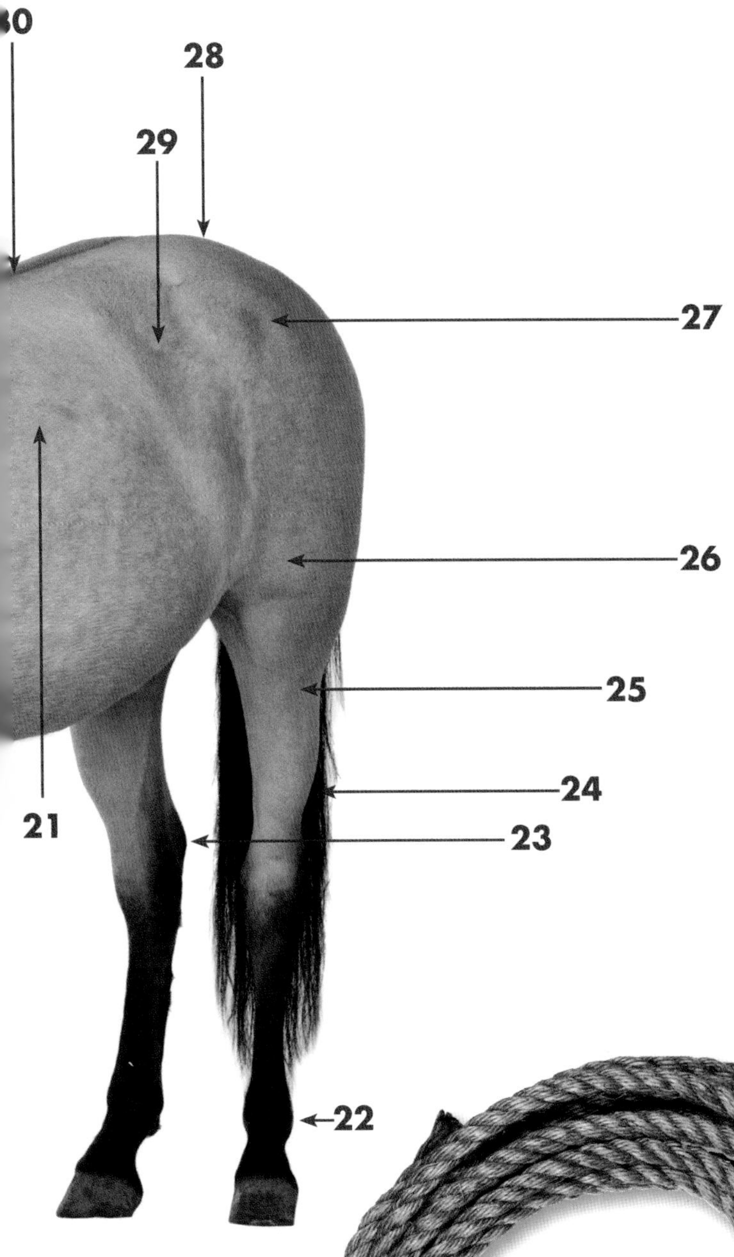

To Find Out More

IN THE LIBRARY

Driscoll , Laura. *Horses*. New York: Grosset & Dunlap, 1997.

Funston, Sylvia. *The Kids' Horse Book.* Toronto: Maple Tree Press, 1993.

Hartley Edwards, Elwyn. *Horses*. New York: Dorling Kindersley, 1993.

Ransford, Sandy. *Horse & Pony Breeds.* Boston: Kingfisher, 2003.

ON THE WEB

Visit our Web site for lots of links about Clydesdales:

www.childsworld.com/links

Note to Parents, Teachers, and Librarians: We routinely check our Web links to make sure they're safe, active sites—so encourage your readers to check them out!

Glossary

bay (BAY) A bay horse is brown with a black mane and tail. Some Clydesdales are bays.

breed (BREED) A breed is a certain type of an animal. Clydesdales are a breed of horse.

carriages (KAYR-uh-jiz) Carriages are wheeled wagons for carrying people. Clydesdales were often used to pull carriages..

chestnut (CHEST-nut) A chestnut horse is reddish brown with a brown mane and tail. Some Clydesdales are chestnuts.

draft horses (DRAFT HOR-sez) Draft horses are used to pull loads. Clydesdales are some of the biggest draft horses.

foal (FOHL) A foal is a baby horse. Clydesdale foals grow quickly.

gait (GAYT) A gait is a way of walking or stepping. Clydesdales have a showy, high-stepping gait.

roan (ROHN) Roan horses are a solid color with a few white hairs. Some Clydesdales are roans.

withers (WIH-thurz) The withers is the highest part of a horse's back. Clydesdales are often 6 feet (almost 2 meters) tall at the withers.

Index